Dusk's Palette

Poems Painted in Twilight and Moonlight

Radhika Saraogi

India | USA | UK

Made with ❤ on the BookLeaf Publishing Platform
www.bookleafpub.in
www.bookleafpub.com

Dedication

For those who find solace in quiet hues of twilight and
the gentle glow of the moon,
who see beauty in every shifting cloud and every fading
sun,
and who know that some stories are best told in the
colours of dusk and the whispers of starlight.

Preface

There's a quiet magic that unfolds as the sun
dips below the horizon and the sky transforms.
This book is a collection of poems born from
those ephemeral moments -- when the day
bids farewell in hues of gold, pink, and violet,
and the night embraces us under a soft, silvery
glow.

Sunsets, clouds, and the moon are constants in
a world of change, silently speaking to anyone
who pauses to listen. They remind us of life's
fleeting beauty, its gentle rhythms, and the
cycles of light and darkness we all face. these
poems were written as whispers to the sky,
reflections on the familiar yet endlessly
captivating dance of dusk and dawn.

Acknowledgements

Creating this collection has been a journey of capturing fleeting moments and turning them into lasting words. My deepest gratitude goes to those who inspired this work -- those who pause to look up, who find beauty in a golden sunset, a gathering of clouds, or the quiet light of the moon. Your appreciation for the world's simplest wonders encouraged me to put these thoughts to paper.

To my friends and family, thank you for your endless encouragement and belief in my vision. Your support lights my way as surely as any sunset or moonrise.

Lastly, to the readers who hold this book in their hands -- thank you for walking with me into the twilight, for embracing the in-betweens, and for sharing in the beauty of dusk's gentle palette. May these pages bring you as much joy in reading as they did in writing.

Instagram: @artistrybyradhikaa

WINGS AND THE MOON

Under the sky, where the world feels light,
A crescent moon shines, so calm, so bright.
A bird in flight, chasing dreams untold,
In the soft blue air, where stories unfold.

Wings in the wind, the moon in sight,
Dancing together through the fading light.
The Sky's an ocean, so vast, so free,
Where the bird and the moon make poetry.

Silent whispers in the evening breeze,
The day fades away with such sweet ease.
The moon calls softly, a silver glow,
And the bird flies higher, in the flow.

Wings in the wind, the moon in sight,
Dancing together through the fading light.
The Sky's an ocean, so vast, so free,
Where the bird and the moon make poetry.

And in the stillness, there's a quiet song,
Of how the night and day belong.
The moon waits patiently, while birds take flight,
Together they soar, into the night.

Wings in the wind, the moon in sight,
Dancing together through the fading light.
The Sky's an ocean, so vast, so free,
Where the bird and the moon make poetry.

In the endless sky, they'll always be,
A timeless dance, for all to see.

WINGS IN THE SKY

In the quiet of the evening,
The sky whispers soft and slow,
Moon up high, just a sliver of light,
While the clouds put on their show.

Birds take flight, they glide so free
In the golden hues, so gracefully,
Up above, where dreams align,
Wings in the sky, crossing time.

Fly away, into the blue,
Where the world is wide, and the skies are true,
With the moon so far, and the clouds so near,
We'll chase the stars, without fear.
Wings In the sky, we soar tonight,
Carried by the winds of light.

The horizon's painted with sunsets grace,
A fleeting moment, a soft embrace,
As we rise like the birds, heart in hand,

Drifting away from the crowded land.

Up we go, in endless skies,
Where the silence speaks, where freedom lies,
In this quiet, we come alive,
With every beat, we'll thrive and rise.

Fly away, into the blue,
Where the world is wide, and the skies are true,
With the moon so far, and the clouds so near,
We'll chase the stars, without fear.
Wings In the sky, we soar tonight,
Carried by the winds of light.

We leave behind the weight of the ground,
Up here, where only dreams are found,
Together we'll dance, in the light of the moon,
Knowing the night will come too soon.

WHISPERS OF THE SHORE

The breeze is soft, the sky so blue,
Waves are calling out to you,
Footsteps fade in golden sand,
As I reach for your hand.

Whispers of the shore, they sing,
Underneath the clouds, we dream,
In this moment, time stands still,
Hearts collide, and oceans fill.

The shadows dance beneath the sun,
A quiet place where we are one,
Lets drift away with every tide,
In the arms of the sea, we'll hide.

Whispers of the shore, they sing,
Underneath the clouds, we dream,
In this moment, time stands still,
Hearts collide, and oceans fill.

We'll leave our worried for behind,
Sail the currents, free our mind,
In the silence, love will bloom,
Like the waves beneath the moon.

Whispers of the shore, they sing,
In the arms of the sea, we cling.

FIRE SKY

The sky's ablaze in crimson light,
Burning through the edge of night.
Im standing here, with flames in sight,
Chasing shadows, chasing time.

Every cloud is glowing bright,
Like embers in a wild flight.
I feel it in the air tonight,
Something's changing, something's right.

It's a fire sky, burning high,
Lighting up the world with its goodbye.
A blaze of gold, a sport in me,
In the fire sky, I'm running free.
Yeah, the fire sky, we ignite,
With every colour in the fading light.
A flame within, we rise and fly,
Underneath the fire sky.

TWILIGHTS QUIET BLAZE

The sky's on fire, a quiet blaze,
Orange hues in twilights haze.
Wishes of the sun's farewell,
In the glowing light we dwell.

YAADON KA SITARA

Aasman ne apne rangon ko saja diya,
Raat aane se pehle, sapna naya diya,
Hawaaon mein mehka hai rang tera,
Chupp gaya suraj, par yaadon ka sitara.

SURAJ KI LAALI

Suraj ki laali me,
Khoya hai yeh manzar,
Leheron se milke,
Dil hai behek raha safar.

PASTEL DREAMS

The sky wears soft pastels tonight,
Brushes of pink in fading light.
A hint of lavender, blue so shy,
Whispers a dream across the sky.

COTTON CLOUDS

Cotton clouds in hues so light,
Paint the dusk, a quiet sight.
The pastel sky, a fleeting view,
Softly speaks in shades of blue.

LAVENDER SKIES

Lavender skies in twilights glow,
With peach and rose that gently flow,
A tender palette, still and shy,
Holds the beauty of goodbye.

A STORY TOLD

The evening blushes soft and sweet,
Pastel skies where day and night meet.
With every shade, a story told,
Of gentle light and colours bold.

UNDER THE DUSKY SKIES

Under the dusky skies,
where the winds whisper secrets and palm trees sway
like overs in a slow dance, our story begins.
A perfect night for destiny to make its move.

A LONE BIRD

A lone bird soars thought the twilight,
As the sky transforms from soft oranges to delicate
purples,
Signalling the peaceful close of a coastal day..

TRANQUIL SUNSET

Tranquil sunset sky with soft orange and golden light,
Sprinkled with birds in flight,
Gently transitioning into dusk,
While the ocean breeze whispers below.

THE SKY IS ART

The sky is art, alive, untamed,
A masterpiece that can't be named.
In this fleeting hour, we see,
The sky's wild heart, forever free.

HALF MOON'S LULLABY

In the sky, a half moon hangs,
Not quite whole, but not less grand.
A sliver of light, soft and bright,
Whispering secrets to the night.

With half its heart in shadow deep,
It cradles stars while the world sleeps,
A crescent smile in the velvet dark,
Leaving on the sky its quiet mark.

It doesn't need to shine complete,
To charm the earth beneath its feet.
For its partial, tender glow,
There's a peace only the half moon knows.

MOONLIT MEMORIES

The moon holds the night, waiting just for you,
In every beam, your memories softly shine through.
When the dawn arrives, carrying your trace,
Until then, the moon quietly weaves dreams in its
embrace.

SUKOON BHARI SHAAM

Sukoon bhari shaam, aur kitab ka saath,
In paloon me bus yu hi behkte rahe hum,
Khule aasman ke talle,
Panno me lipti kahaniyan, kho jaane ki ye shaam.

TUM HO MERE SAATH

Do pal ka tha yeh saath humara,
Shaam dhalti, samundar ka kinara.
Hawaoon mein tha tera pyaar,
Din ko alvida ken rahi thi ye pyaari shaam pyaara.

Chandini raat aur tera intezaar,
Dil se dil tak ka safar hamesha rahega yaadgaar.
Palkon pe sajaaye humne yeh pyaari yaadein,
Har shaam, har pal, tum ho humare saath yun hi
humesha.

SURAJ KO CHHUNE KA SAPNA

Suraj ko chhune ka sapna,
Leheronn se baatein karna,
Dil ke aasman pe khushi ka ujala,
Har pal ko jeena hai bas yahi irada.

Deere dheere chhup raha yeh pal,
Zameen se aasman tak chaayi halchal,
Lehron ki dhun mein hai ek geet naya,
Suraj ke saath milke duniya ko jagaaya.

Suraj ko chhune ka sapnaa,
leheron se baatein karna...

GOLDEN SKIES & ELECTRIC TRAILS

The sky is art, alive, untamed,
A masterpiece that can't be named.
In this fleeting hour, we see,
The sky's wild heart, forever free.